GARRARD COUNTY, KENTUCKY

Tax Lists 1820 & 1828

J. L. DICKSON

In association with

Personal Touch Genealogy
www.PersonalTouchGenealogy.com

and

ETC
ETCETERA
PUBLISHING

www.GenealogyBookPublisher.com

ISBN 978-0-9818351-9-8
Published by Etcetera Publishing LLC — Fort Worth, TX
Printed in the United States of America
First Edition

Please visit **www.PersonalTouchGenealogy.com**
to order this book or see Order Form on page 55.

RECORDS ROOM, Garrard County Courthouse, Lancaster, KY

GARRARD COUNTY, KENTUCKY

1820 Tax List

ABBREVIATION LEGEND

R = River

Cr = Creek

LAN = City of Lancaster Kentucky

NIC = City of Nicholasville Kentucky

GARRARD COUNTY 1820 TAX LIST

Name	Acreage	County	Water Course	Whites Over 21	Blacks Over 16	Total Blacks	Horses	Total Value
Adams George	214	Garrard	Sugar Cr	1	3	5	9	5557
Adams Willis				1		1	2	500
Albow Ann	60	Garrard	Dicks R				3	700
Aldridge James	245	Garrard	Sugar Cr	1	6	11	11	
Aldridge James	42	Garrard	Sugar Cr					10094
Alford Jesse	87	Garrard	Dicks R	1	1	3	5	2220
Alford Morgan	281	Garrard	Dicks R	2	1	3	8	4110
Alford Peyton	106	Garrard	Dicks R	1	2	3	2	2220
Allen John				1			1	100
Allen Joseph				1				
Allen Richard	131	Garrard	Canoe Cr	1			1	1100
Allen Samuel	52	Garrard	Sugar Cr	1	1	1	4	1066
Anderson Cornelus	105	Garrard	Sugar Cr	1			5	950
Anderson Elizabeth	285	Garrard	Sugar Cr		2	7	7	
Anderson Elizabeth	100	Garrard	Sugar Cr					6820
Anderson James				1			1	100
Anderson John				1				
Arnold Absolom	250	Washington	Deep Cr	1		1	3	2175
Arnold Isaac	165	Garrard	Boons Cr	1	1	2	4	3575
Askins Alex				1				
Askins John				1				
Askins Peggy	105	Garrard	Kentucky R		1	4	2	2200
Austin Adam				1			1	50
Austin Adam				1			1	40
Austin James				1			1	100
Back James				1				
Bagley Edward				1			1	50
Bagley Lewis				1			2	80
Baker Beverly				1			1	50
Baker James	150	Garrard	Sugar Cr	1			3	1670
Baker James				1			1	60
Baker Martin	100	Barren	Barren	1	2	3	2	980
Baker Martin				1			2	150
Ball Allen				1			1	50
Ball James	280	Garrard	Dicks R	1	4	4	5	
Ball James	100	Garrard	Dicks R					

GARRARD COUNTY 1820 TAX LIST

Name	Acreage	County	Water Course	Whites Over 21	Blacks Over 16	Total Blacks	Horses	Total Value
Ball James	100	Garrard	Dicks R					
Ball James	250	Garrard	Dicks R					6415
Ball James				1			1	40
Ball John				1			1	50
Ball Mary							2	75
Ballenger Achilles	190	Garrard	Sugar Cr	1	4	10	5	
Ballenger Achilles	200	Adair						5500
Ballenger Henry	171 1/4	Garrard	Sugar Cr	1	1	2	2	2802
Banks Garrard	100	Garrard	Sugar Cr	1	1	4	4	2450
Banks John	134 1/2	Garrard	Sugar Cr	1		3	4	2470
Banks Linn	70	Garrard	Sugar Cr	1			1	760
Banks William	100	Garrard	Sugar Cr	1	3	3	7	2500
Banton George W.				1			1	100
Barker Richard				1				
Barlow Nancy	250	Garrard	Boons Cr		2	7	3	4725
Barnete Eddy	123 1/2	Garrard	Sugar Cr	1	2	3	1	1711
Barnett John	70	Garrard	Sugar Cr	1			2	780
Bayley James				1				
Bealer George				1			3	125
Bealkles John				1		2	1	1670
Beasley Elijah				1	3	6	3	2270
Beasley Thomas				1	1	3	2	1100
Beckham William				1	1	3	2	1600
Belt Richard	100	Garrard	Gilbert Cr	1	3	6	3	3425
Best Banks				1				
Best John				1			2	100
Best Samuel	400	Pulaski		1			2	650
Bivens John				1			2	50
Blackwell George				1			1	30
Blackwile Robert				1			3	150
Blackwill Zachariah				1			1	50
Bland Charles	190	Garrard	Dicks R	1	1	1	7	
Bland Charles	50	Garrard	Dicks R					4345
Bland Thomas					1	1	1	2100
Blanton Joshua	80	Garrard	Kentucky River	1	2	2	2	1670

GARRARD COUNTY 1820 TAX LIST

Name	Acreage	County	Water Course	Whites Over 21	Blacks Over 16	Total Blacks	Horses	Total Value
Blonton Elijah	100	Garrard	Kentucky River	1			3	800
Bornes James C.				1			1	100
Bosalloy Peter D.	44	Garrard	Kentucky River	1				
Bourne Francis				1			1	25
Bourne John				1		1	1	520
Bowman George	470	Garrard	Kentucky River	1	15	24	11	13385
Boyd Andrew				1			1	100
Brady John				1			2	100
Brady John				1				
Bright James	123	Garrard	Dicks R	1	3	8	5	4495
Bright Thomas	75	Garrard	Dicks R	1	1	2	7	2425
Brown Amalia	145	Garrard	Sugar Cr	1	1	3	3	3340
Brown Beverly	54 1/2	Garrard	Sugar Cr	1			3	665
Brown Henry	80	Garrard	Dicks R	1	1	1	5	1750
Brown Henry	121	Garrard	Sugar Cr	1			3	1532
Brown James				1				
Brown John	200	Garrard	Canoe Cr	1			2	1070
Brown Joseph A.				1				
Brown Leroy	179	Garrard	Sugar Cr	1			4	1990
Brown Robert	198	Garrard	Canoe Cr	1			3	1070
Brown Samuel				1			1	30
Brown Thomas				1				
Brown William	154	Garrard	Sugar Cr	1	2	2	4	
Brown William	143	Garrard	White Oak Cr					
Brown William	25	Mercer	Kentucky River					3680
Brown William	34	Garrard	White Oak Cr	1	1	2	1	1420
Brown William				1			5	200
Brownes Amelia					9	17	9	6000
Brownes Noah				1	2	4	3	1400
Bruce R. P.	341	Garrard	Sugar Cr	1	1	1	1	
Bruce R. P.	254	Garrard	Sugar Cr					10720

GARRARD COUNTY 1820 TAX LIST

Name	Acreage	County	Water Course	Whites Over 21	Blacks Over 16	Total Blacks	Horses	Total Value
Bruce Richard P.	100	Garrard	Sugar Cr					
Bryan Wilcllis				1	1	1	1	650
Bryan William								
Bryant Edmond	112	Garrard	Boons Cr	1	1	2	2	2400
Bryant George	100	Garrard		1	2	7	3	4200
Bryant John	250	Garrard	Sugar Cr	2	3	9	5	
Bryant John	500	Rockcastle	Dicks R					
Bryant John	200	Rockcastle	Rockcastle					
Bryant John	40	Garrard	Sugar Cr					8480
Bryant Johnathon				1		1	1	580
Bryant Samuel	220	Garrard	Dicks R	1	2	3	6	4450
Bryant Thomas	100	Garrard	Boons Cr	1			2	1580
Buck Enoch				1			2	130
Buck Joseph	157	Garrard	Kentucky R	1			4	1259
Buford John	97 3/4	Garrard	Gilbert Cr	1	4	6	7	3318
Buford Thomas				1	8	11	2	11750
Bunch George				1				
Bunch James				1				
Bunch John	95	Garrard	Dicks R	1			8	
Bunch John	35	Garrard	Sugar Cr					3125
Bunch John	113	Garrard	Sugar Cr	1	1	2	4	1966
Bunch Michael				1			1	50
Burdett Enoch	230	Garrard	Boons Cr	1	1	1	3	4020
Burdett Gracy	569	Garrard			7	13	9	13365
Burdett Hiram				1			1	60
Burdett Joseph	350	Garrard	Boons Cr	1	8	12	11	
Burdett Joseph	1000	Lincoln	Buck Cr					
Burdett Joseph	100	Gallatin	Ohio					11440
Burdett Nelson	600	Garrard	Dicks R					
Burdett Nelson	400	Lincoln	Buck R					6800
Burdett Nelson							1	100
Burdett Wesley				1	1	1	1	685
Burke Floyd				1				
Burks Thompson	100	Garrard	Kentucky R	1			2	440
Burnside Robert	315	Garrard	Sugar Cr	1	4	12	8	8430
Burnsides James	227	Garrard	Sugar Cr	1	3	11	6	6229

4

GARRARD COUNTY 1820 TAX LIST

Name	Acreage	County	Water Course	Whites Over 21	Blacks Over 16	Total Blacks	Horses	Total Value
Burnsides John	170	Garrard	Sugar Cr	1	2	3	7	3740
Byans John	109	Garrard	Dicks R	1	2	6	4	3465
Byons Edmond	100	Garrard	Boons Cr	1	1	9	5	
Byons Edmond	15	Garrard	Sugar Cr					5000
Caisey Levy				1			1	50
Calleron Absalom	113	Garrard	Dicks R	1	1	3	6	2000
Calley James				1			1	50
Campbell Moses	24	Garrard	Gilbert Cr	1			2	228
Carter Joseph					1	1	1	890
Carter Solomon				1			1	830
Cays Charles				1			1	40
Cays John				1			1	60
Cays John				1				
Cays Mary	275	Garrard	Canoe Cr				4	1800
Cecil James	140	Garrard	White Oak Cr	1	1	4	3	2150
Cecil John				1			1	60
Cecil Richard				1			1	50
Chaplain Baley					1	3	2	875
Chauder Dennis				1				
Chisman Laya				1			1	30
Clands Abner				1			3	200
Clanke Reuben				1			1	70
Clarke David				1			5	200
Clarke Robert				1			1	35
Clemmond Francis				1			2	80
Clemmons George	150	Garrard	Canoe Cr	1			4	1320
Clemmons James		Garrard	Sugar Cr	1			2	80
Clemmons Thomas				1			5	220
Clemmons William				1				
Clemons Francis	90	Garrard	Sugar Cr	1			3	1060
Clemons Stephen				1				
Clouke John						1	1	75
Collier Aaron	100	Garrard	Davey Cr	1	1	4	3	2150
Collier Alexander	3 3/4	Garrard	Sugar Cr	1			1	75

GARRARD COUNTY 1820 TAX LIST

Name	Acreage	County	Water Course	Whites Over 21	Blacks Over 16	Total Blacks	Horses	Total Value
Collier Alexander (children)	25							250
Collier Jacob				1				
Collier John	90	Garrard	Sugar Cr	1			3	1230
Collier Moses	208	Garrard	Canoe Cr	1		1	3	2414
Collier Robert	141 1/4	Garrard	Sugar Cr	1			5	
Collier Robert	155	Garrard	Sugar Cr					2670
Cooke Peyton	150	Garrard	Sugar Cr	1			4	
Cooke Peyton	100	Garrard	Sugar Cr					2200
Cooke William	5	Garrard	Boons Cr		1	2	3	19000
Cooke William				1				
Coones Henry								
Cooper William	150	Garrard	Mans Cr	3	1	2	4	
Cosby James D.				1		1	2	400
Crabb John	261 3/4	Garrard	Dicks R	1	5	11	9	9226
Craig Frederich				1			2	200
Craig John	64	Garrard	Sugar Cr	1			3	890
Critchfield John	175	Garrard	Davey Cr	1	1	3	2	1885
Critchfield Mordeeai				1			1	75
Critchfield Nicholen				1				
Crockett John	110	Garrard	Sugar Cr	1	1	1	6	1650
Cumpton Ben	74	Garrard	Dicks R	1	2	6	3	2394
Darnell George				1			2	75
David Solomon				1			3	100
Davis Asual				1			2	100
Davis Asual Sr.	686	Garrard	Dicks R	1	5	9	7	
Davis Asual Sr.	74 3/4							14913
Davis Edward				1			5	200
Davis Wedward				1				
Davis William				1	3	7	5	2275
Delph Elijah				1			1	30
Dennis Elisha	94	Garrard	Sugar Cr	1			1	1000
Denton Henry	232	Knox	Robinson Cr	1			1	611
Denton John	140	Garrard	Sugar Cr	1	5	16	4	6330
Denton John	100	Garrard	Sugar Cr	1	2	4	4	2810

GARRARD COUNTY 1820 TAX LIST

Name	Acreage	County	Water Course	Whites Over 21	Blacks Over 16	Total Blacks	Horses	Total Value
Denton Josiah	130	Garrard	Sugar Cr	1			1	750
Denton William				1			1	100
Dismukes Iams	35	Garrard	Kentucky R		1	1	1	450
Dismukes William	64	Garrard	Sugar Cr	1		1	3	884
Donell William				1			2	100
Downing John	157	Garrard	Kentucky R	1	2	3	3	
Downing John	100	Cumberland	Marabow Cr					3070
Downing William	181	Garrard	Sugar Cr	1		1	1	2300
Duggins Elizabeth	117	Garrard	Sugar Cr				2	1220
Duggins John				1			1	50
Duglass Nathan	78	Garrard	Gilbert Cr	1	1	5	5	2834
Duglass Samuel				1				
Duncan William	158	Garrard	Sugar Cr	1	3	7	6	4846
Dunn Augustine	219 1/4	Garrard	Dicks R	1	8	17	13	
Dunn Augustine	10	Garrard	White Oak Cr					9803
Dunn Benjamin	249 1/2	Garrard	Dicks R	1	7	10	10	7850
Dunn Eramus	70	Garrard	Boons Cr	1	1			1700
Dunn John	50	Garrard	Boons Cr	1	1	1	3	1575
Dunn John	150	Garrard	Dicks R	3	4	10	12	
Dunn John								6360
Dunn John A.	100	Garrard	Dicks R	1	2	5	4	
Dunn John A.	100	Barren	Barren R					3600
Dunn John A.	100	Rockcastle	Rockcastle					
Dunn Walter	44	Garrard	Boons Cr	1	1	1	3	2025
Dunn William	200	Garrard	Boons Cr	1	7	19	12	10000
Dunn William	165	Garrard	Dicks R	1	4	6	6	4280
Eason John				1			2	125
Edmondson Clary	212	Garrard	Canoe Cr	1	3	8	5	4984
Edmondson John				1			1	100
Edwards Ambrose				1			3	125
Edwards John				1			1	30
Egerton Benjamin	200	Garrard	Dicks R	1			1	1700
Egerton Benjamin	34 1/2	Garrard	Kentucky R	1			1	395

GARRARD COUNTY 1820 TAX LIST

Name	Acreage	County	Water Course	Whites Over 21	Blacks Over 16	Total Blacks	Horses	Total Value
Egerton Benjamin J.	6	Garrard	Dicks R	1	1	2	1	710
Egerton James				1	1	1	2	770
Egerton John				1			2	75
Egerton William				1			1	30
Elliott Essey				1			1	100
Elliott George	110	Garrard	Dicks R	1			5	1270
Ellis Leondas								
England Augustus				1			1	50
England James	84	Garrard	Dicks R	1			4	912
England Spotwood				1				
Erames Allen	83	Garrard	Davis Cr	1	1	1	2	1300
Evans Ambrose				1			1	30
Evans John				1	1	4	2	2025
Evans John Jr.				1			1	50
Evans Joseph	130	Garrard	White Oak Cr	1	1	3	3	3160
Everts Gustuves								
Fainley John				1				
Fainley Peter	93	Garrard	Dicks R	1	1	2	4	1916
Floyd Christopher				1			1	100
Floyd George	100	Garrard	Clecs Cr	1	3	9	3	4660
Floyd John	319 1/2	Garrard	Sugar Cr	2	9	15	6	7745
Floyd Thomas				1	1	2	2	650
Ford Reuben				1			1	50
Ford Timothy	105	Garrard	Kentucky R	1			2	690
Ford William				1			1	60
Fowler Moore				1				
Frances Robert				1			2	80
French Hishn								
Frey Joshua	800	Garrard	Dicks R	2	5	8	4	
Frey Joshua	473	Jessamine	Hickman					
Frey Joshua	292	Mercer	Cam R					23050
Furney Betsey	33	Garrard	Dicks R	1			3	330
Furney John	66 3/4	Garrard	Dicks R	1			3	817
Gates Elijah								

GARRARD COUNTY 1820 TAX LIST

Name	Acreage	County	Water Course	Whites Over 21	Blacks Over 16	Total Blacks	Horses	Total Value
George James	286	Garrard	G. Cr	1	7	10	9	
George James	33							9761
George Robert				1		2	1	830
Gibson James				1			1	50
Gibson Silas				1				
Gibson William	115	Garrard	Dicks R	2	4	13	3	5230
Gilbert Henry				1			1	25
Gill Eramus							2	130
Gill John	193	Garrard	Boons Cr	1	7	17	10	
Gill John	93							12625
Gill Samuel				1		7	9	
Gill Samuel				1				
Gill William							1	50
Goldberry Martin	15	Garrard	G. Cr	1				155
Gosser Peter				1			1	30
Graham Elizabeth	66 1/3	Garrard	Sugar Cr		1	5	1	2473
Graham John					1		2	250
Graham Luke	4 1/2	Garrard	Sugar Cr	1			4	221
Graham Moses				1			1	30
Green Benjamin				1			1	50
Green Hansom				1			1	60
Green Loab	40	Garrard	Kentucky R	1			2	370
Green Zachriah	140	Garrard	Sugar Cr	1	2	2	2	2000
Gresson Robert				1			1	60
Gribby Samuel				1			1	50
Grider Nellie	27	Garrard	White Oak Cr				2	
Grider Nellie	200	Barren	Barren R					1116
Grissham Isaac				1			1	25
Gromer John	63			1	1	1	3	1254
Groom Jesse				1				1500
Hackney Samuel				1			1	30
Hadrick Joseph				1			1	
Hagen Bendict				1	1	1	1	710
Haggard Rico				1				
Hale Randal	115	Garrard	Sugar Cr	1	1	1	8	

9

GARRARD COUNTY 1820 TAX LIST

Name	Acreage	County	Water Course	Whites Over 21	Blacks Over 16	Total Blacks	Horses	Total Value
Hale Randal	170	Pulaski	W.O. Cr					2000
Hall David				1			2	120
Hamilton Kelley	75	Garrard	Dicks R		1	6	3	2500
Hamm John	335	Garrard	Gilberts Cr		2	8	8	8625
Hammons Hopper								13500
Hampton George				1				
Hancock Jesse				1			2	100
Hancock Stacey	80	Garrard	Dicks R		1	1	2	730
Harbin Edward				1			3	125
Harbin Samuel				1			1	30
Harmon Jacob	199	Garrard	Dicks R	1	1	2	3	1925
Harmon Reese				1			2	75
Hatchel Thomas				1		1	2	400
Hedrick Jacob				1				
Hedrick Joseph	97	Garrard	Dicks R	1	3	6	8	4000
Hedrick Joseph	80	Garrard	Dicks R					
Hedrick Peter	125	Garrard	White Oak Cr	1			9	2475
Henderson John	106 1/2	Garrard	Dicks R	1	1	1	7	1350
Henry William	118	Garrard	Sugar Cr	1	2	3	2	2431
Herdon John				1			2	120
Herring Augustine				1			1	75
Herring George	109	Garrard	Dicks R	1	1	2	3	2165
Herring Terrill				1		1	1	500
Herring Thomas	450	Garrard	Dicks R	1	5	12	6	
Herring Thomas	30	Garrard	Dicks R					9890
Hersey Meridith	195	Garrard	White Oak Cr	1	3	8	6	4850
Hicks (Melvin ?)				1			1	40
Hicks Cornelius				1			1	50
Hicks Fleming				1			1	50
Hicks Joseph	146	Garrard	Sugar Cr	1			1	850
Hicks Nathaniel				1			2	70
Hicks William				1			1	40
Higgins Luciss								
Hill Jesse	217	Garrard	Sugar Cr	1	1	1	3	2506

GARRARD COUNTY 1820 TAX LIST

Name	Acreage	County	Water Course	Whites Over 21	Blacks Over 16	Total Blacks	Horses	Total Value
Hill John	57	Garrard	Sugar Cr	1			2	630
Hill Samuel				1			2	100
Himes Solomon B.	43	Garrard	Dicks R	1				215
Hogan Elizabeth	88	Garrard	Dicks R		1	1	2	
Hogan Elizabeth	100	Rockcastle	Rockcastle					1544
Hogan John	75	Garrard & Jessamine	Kentucky R	1	1	7	3	
Hogan John	100	Rockcastle	Kentucky R					3630
Hogan Samuel	109	Garrard	Dicks R	1	1	3	2	
Hogan Samuel	100	Rockcastle	Dicks R					2517
Holtzclaw Abner	79	Garrard	Dicks R	1			2	1028
Holtzclaw Elijah	51 1/2	Garrard	Sugar Cr	1			1	545
Holtzclaw Jacob	100	Garrard	Dicks R	1	1	2	7	2350
Holtzclaw James				1				
Holtzclaw Jesse	33	Garrard	Dicks R	1			2	539
Holtzclaw Martin	27	Gararrd	Dicks R	1			3	255
Hopewood Christopher	41	Garrard	Dicks R	1			6	355
Hopper John								
Hopper Joseph					2	2	1	1650
Hoskins William	412	Garrard	Dicks R	1	5	13	18	12280
House John				1			2	80
House Mathias	244	Garrard	Dicks R	1			5	2640
Huddleton Henry	150	Garrard	Sugar Cr	1			5	2000
Huffman Edmund				1			1	70
Huffman Henry	40	Garrard	Sugar Cr	1			3	600
Huffman Henry C.				1			1	60
Huffman Henry C.				1			2	100
Huffman Huston				1			1	20
Huffman James				1			1	60
Huffman John	40	Garrard	Sugar Cr	1			3	550
Huffman John				1			2	150
Huffman John	50	Garrard	Sugar Cr	1				400
Huffman William	115	Garrard	Sugar Cr	1	1	2	4	2250
Huffman William					1	2	4	3750
Hughes William				1				

GARRARD COUNTY 1820 TAX LIST

Name	Acreage	County	Water Course	Whites Over 21	Blacks Over 16	Total Blacks	Horses	Total Value
Hunter Samuel	100			1			4	150
Hutcherson John	402	Garrard	Sugar Cr	1	1	4	7	
Hutcherson John	88	Garrard	Sugar Cr					
Hutcherson John	66	Garrard	Sugar Cr					7024
Hutchinson Randel				1			1	50
Hutchmon Josiah				1			1	80
Hutchmon Phillip	50	Garrard	Dicks R	1			1	675
Hutchmon Spencer				1				
Huton Benjamin	97	Garrard	Sugar Cr	1	2	5	7	3314
Huton William				1			1	50
Hutson George	108	Garrard	Sugar Cr	1			2	1130
Irvin Ananias				1		1	3	500
Irvin Dory				1			2	120
Irvin Williamson				1		1	3	430
Ison Charles				1			1	50
Ison Charles	100	Garrard	Dicks R	1			1	650
Ison James	111	Garrard	Dicks R	1	2	4	2	2216
Ison James	100	Garrard	Dicks R	1	2	8	4	3000
Ison James				1			1	60
Ison John	170	Garrard	Dicks R	1	1	2	3	1970
Ison John				1			1	30
Ison Michael				1				
Ison Nelson	45	Garrard	Dicks R	1			2	600
Ison Nelson	45	Garrard	Dicks R					
Ison William				1	2	5	3	1665
Ison William				1			1	40
Jackman George	196 1/2	Garrard	Dicks R	1				2947
Jackman Samuel	211	Garrard	White Oak Cr	1	4	8	5	6977
Jackson Martin				1				100
Jamison Alexander	62 1/2	Garrard	Canoe Cr	1			2	560
Jeffers William	175	Garrard	Dicks R	1			4	2300
Jenikins William	400	Casey	Fishing Cr	1			4	
Jenkins David				1			3	125
Jenkins Henry				1		1	2	1350
Jenkins Jonathan	424	Garrard	Kentucky R	1	6	10	5	8690

GARRARD COUNTY 1820 TAX LIST

Name	Acreage	County	Water Course	Whites Over 21	Blacks Over 16	Total Blacks	Horses	Total Value
Jenkins Jonathan				1			1	50
Jenkins William	50	Casey	Fishing Cr					875
Jennings Alex A.				1			1	30
Jennings Augustine	231 1/4	Garrard	Dicks R	1	3	10	5	6031
Jennings Baylor	144 1/4	Garrard	Sugar Cr	1	1	4	2	2210
Jennings Henley B.				1			2	120
Jennings John B.	115	Garrard	White Oak Cr	1	1	3	4	
Jennings John B.	60	Garrard	Canoe Cr					2085
Johnston John	100	Garrard	Sugar Cr	1	2	5	2	2700
Jones (Stoches ?)				1			1	75
Jones Fracis	150	Garrard	Sugar Cr		2	2	4	2250
Jones John	120	Garrard	Sugar Cr	1	4	8	1	4170
Kemper Arthur				1	1	2	2	880
Kemper Bendall				1			1	80
Kemper George				1	1	1	2	650
Kemper John	200	Garrard	Boons Cr	1	3	12	5	
Kemper John	1550	Madison	Station Cr					6957
Kemper John				1			1	80
Kemper John	100	Garrard	Dicks R	1	1	1	3	1120
Kemper Thornton	200	Madison	Clear Cr	1	3	6	3	5350
Kemper William	108 1/2	Garrard	White Oak Cr	1	2	2	4	1878
Kenningham Amelia					4	7	8	2925
Kidd Richard				1				
King Ibzan	70	Garrard	Dicks R	1			2	800
King William				1			2	50
Lamm Molley	102 1/2	Garrard	Dicks R		2	3	6	
Lamm Molley	283	Henry	Six Mile					3354
Lane Johnston								
Lane Laskin	43			1			1	35
Lane William				1			1	50
Lapsley John A.	327	Garrard	Gilberts Cr	1	7	10	4	
Lapsley John A.	200	Garrard	Gilberts Cr					10411
Leosure Nathan	43	Garrard	Dicks R	1			3	500
Letcher Alex				1	2	5	5	1400

GARRARD COUNTY 1820 TAX LIST

Name	Acreage	County	Water Course	Whites Over 21	Blacks Over 16	Total Blacks	Horses	Total Value
Letcher Benjamin	150	Garrard	Gilberts Cr	1	7	17	9	
Letcher Benjamin	40	Garrard	White Oak Cr					9250
Letcher Robert					1	1	5	3000
Letcher Rowland	25	Jessamine	Hickman	1		1	6	2725
Letcher Stephen					1	1	2	3200
Letcher Stephen					1	5	10	4880
Lethout Robert				1			2	80
Lewis Samuel	78 3/4	Garrard	Gilberts Cr	1			7	1233
Loyd Moses				1			2	50
Lusk John	55	Garrard	Sugar Cr	1			2	655
Lusk William	85	Garrard	Sugar Cr	1			1	1325
Lusk William				1	1	1	1	550
Madduac Alfred				1			1	80
Madduac Thomas B.	173	Garrard	Gilberts Cr	1	2	7	5	3630
Manfield Will	444	Garrard	Canoe Cr	1			2	4900
Marksbury Isaac	135	Garrard	Sugar Cr	1	2	8	5	4325
Marksbury William	125	Garrard	Sugar Cr	1	1	7	3	3890
Marthon John				1				
Martin Nimrod				1				
Martin William				1			1	50
Mason Benjamin	160	Garrard	Sugar Cr	1	7	12	6	
Mason Benjamin	266	Garrard	Gilberts Cr					16260
Mason John				1			1	50
Mayfield James	97	Garrard	Sugar Cr	1		1	2	1500
McClan Frederick				1				
McCormack Elizabeth	60	Garrard	Dicks R					300
McCoy Daniel	142	Garrard	Dicks R	2	2	2	20	
McCoy Daniel	100	Garrard	Dicks R					4236
McCoy Kenneth				1			1	100
McCoy Kenneth								1350
McDaniel Anquish	60	Garrard		1	1	3	2	1020
McKee James				1	1	1	2	
McKee Samuel	60	Garrard	Boons Cr	2	2	7	6	

GARRARD COUNTY 1820 TAX LIST

Name	Acreage	County	Water Course	Whites Over 21	Blacks Over 16	Total Blacks	Horses	Total Value
McKee Samuel	1666	Wayne						
McKee Samuel	180	Garrard	Dicks R					
McKee Samuel	500	Adair	Wolf					
McKee Samuel	250	Adair	Wolf					
McKee Samuel	500	Adair	Wolf					
McKee Samuel	250	Adair	Wolf					10139
McKee Samuel	580	Garrard	Boons Cr					
McKee Samuel	1300	Green	Robertson					
McKee Samuel	2000	Bath	Salt Cr					13500
McLear Philip				1				
McLin Henry	50	Garrard	Sugar Cr	1			1	675
McLin John				1			1	50
McMutry Alex	250	Garrard	Kentucky R	1	6	14	7	
McMutry Alex	194	Garrard	Kentucky R					
McMutry Alex	145	Garrard	Kentucky R					
McMutry Alex	114	Garrard	Kentucky R					9600
McMutry Samuel	101	Mercer						1010
McQuie Andrew				1			1	100
McQuie John				1	7	12	3	4900
McQuie William				1	3	4	1	2650
McQuie William V. A.	466	Garrard	Kentucky R	2	12	23	11	
McQuie William V. A.	233	Jessamine	Kentucky R					16426
Menhon John				1	2	4	2	1500
Menhon R.F.V.B.	22	Garrard	Dicks R					2200
Menhon R.F.V.B.								
Merhon Andrew	255 1/4	Garrard	Gilberts Cr	1	7	16	9	8875
Merhon Berkett				1				
Merhon Cornelious				1	1	3	1	820
Merhon Robert								
Merritt John				1			1	80
Merritt Richard	114	Garrard		1			4	1280
Mershon Furman				1			1	70
Middleton Isaac				1			2	100
Middleton Martin				1			2	100

GARRARD COUNTY 1820 TAX LIST

Name	Acreage	County	Water Course	Whites Over 21	Blacks Over 16	Total Blacks	Horses	Total Value
Miller Jacob				1			1	50
Miller Samuel							5	750
Moberly Benjamin	46 1/2	Garrard	Boons Cr	1	1	4	4	2067
Moberly Edward	80	Garrard	Gilberts Cr	1			4	1200
Moberly Joab	68 3/4	Garrard	Gilberts Cr	1			5	1123
Moberly John				1			2	100
Montgomery Esther	107	Garrard	Clear Cr			2	5	2320
Montgomery James				1			1	50
Morrison Allen				1			1	60
Mosett Peter				1			2	100
Moss Peyton				1			1	75
Moss William	125	Garrard	White Oak Cr	1			2	800
Mouzy Henry	137 3/4	Garrard	Gilberts Cr	1	5	14	12	7215
Mullins Beverly				1			1	120
Mullins Samuel	25 3/4	Garrard	Dicks R	2	6	20	5	11440
Mullins Thomas				1	2	4	3	1400
Myers Isaac	414 1/2	Garrard	Dicks R	1	5	10	15	7718
Myers Lewis	384 1/2	Garrard	Clear Cr	1	9	22	10	
Myers Lewis	400	Lincoln	Green R					
Myers Lewis	750	Ohio	Yellow R					
Myers Lewis	100	Ohio	Island					
Myers Lewis	50	Ohio	Island					
Myers Lewis	50	Ohio	Island					18542
Myers Lucy							2	75
Nailer Edward				1			3	150
Nailer Samuel	40	Garrard	Sugar Cr	1			2	500
Napper Rainey				1			1	25
Nelson Thomas	15	Garrard	White Oak Cr	1	1	2	4	3417
Nevis James H.								
Newton Nanaff	25	Garrard	Kentucky R				1	200
Newton Samuel								
Newton Walter				1	1	2	3	1100
Noel Moses	100	Garrard	Dicks R	1	3	6	4	
Noel Moses	61	Garrard	Sugar Cr					4210

GARRARD COUNTY 1820 TAX LIST

Name	Acreage	County	Water Course	Whites Over 21	Blacks Over 16	Total Blacks	Horses	Total Value
Noel Musker	94	Garrard	Sugar Cr	1			3	1045
Oatman George				1		1	1	675
Oatman Peter	100	Garrard	Boons Cr	1			1	2100
Obannon David	261	Garrard	Boons Cr	1	4	6	4	5215
Obannon Selvestor				1			1	100
Onstott David				1			1	50
Onstott Nicholas	116	Garrard	County	1			3	1260
Owsley William	370	Garrard	White Oak Cr	1	5	13	7	
Owsley William	33	Garrard	White Oak Cr					14730
Parker Charles	173 1/4	Garrard	Sugar Cr	1	1	1	4	2422
Parkes Thomas	147	Garrard	Sugar Cr	2			3	1887
Parks Allen				1				
Parks Levi				1				
Parks William	165	Garrard	Sugar Cr	1			10	2100
Patrick Alex				1			3	6000
Pawling John L.				1		1		300
Payne James				1			1	25
Payne John				1			1	25
Perkins (Morry?)	180	Garrard	Dicks R		6	8	3	4670
Perkins Edmond	240	Garrard	Dicks R	1	27	16	6	
Perkins Edmond	85	Garrard	Dicks R					
Perkins Edmond	80	Garrard	Dicks R					
Perkins Edmond	150	Mercer	Dicks R					
Perkins Edmond	800	Estill	Kentucky R					
Perkins Edmond	25	Madison	Otter Cr					
Perkins Edmond	1000	Rockcastle	Round Stone					9000
Perkins John				1	1	1		650
Perkins Joseph						1	1	420
Peyton Edwin	135	Garrard	Gilberts Cr	1	3	6	5	4055
Phillips Harrison				1			1	50
Phillips Issac	84 3/4	Garrard	Sugar Cr	1			1	1137
Phillips John	100	Garrard	Sugar Cr	1			1	1050
Poe William				1			2	150

GARRARD COUNTY 1820 TAX LIST

Name	Acreage	County	Water Course	Whites Over 21	Blacks Over 16	Total Blacks	Horses	Total Value
Pollard (Gmeand ?)							1	
Pollard Absalon	170	Garrard	Sugar Cr	1	2	6	5	3425
Pollard Greenville				1	1	3	3	1075
Pollard John								
Pollard Reuben				1				
Pollard Stanton				1			1	60
Pope Alemander	150	Garrard	Dicks R	1	5	12	5	5775
Pope James				1	2	3	1	1410
Pope Thomas				1			1	100
Pope Thomas	125	Garrard	Dicks R	1	7	11	6	5000
Pope William	71	Garrard	Dicks R	1	2	3	4	2273
Porr William	200	Garrard	Kentucky R	1	1	2	3	2135
Porr William	125	Garrard	Kentucky R			1	2	1025
Potter Nathaniel	125	Garrard	Sugar Cr	1			3	1630
Potts Samuel				1			1	80
Preston Enoch	100	Garrard		1			1	550
Proctor Uriah	152			1	4	8	5	4664
Protor Thomas							2	3175
Pruton William				1			1	35
Pulliam Absalom	125	Garrard	Dicks R	1	5	7	7	5525
Pulliam Benjamin				1			1	50
Pulliam John A.	74 3/4	Garrard	Kentucky R	1	1	4	4	1623
Pulliam William	133	Garrard	White Oak Cr	1		1	2	2455
Pulliam William W.	110	Garrard	Dicks R	1	3	3	4	3400
Pulliam Woodrow	67			1	3	5	3	3055
Ramsey Alex		Garrard	Gilberts Cr	1			3	100
Ramsey Edmond	67	Garrard	Gilberts Cr	1		1	3	1145
Ramsey John	124			1			2	1000
Ramsey Larkin	93	Garrard	Gilberts Cr	1	3	6	5	
Ramsey Larkin	52	Garrard	Gilberts Cr					
Ramsey Larkin	465	Bracken	Licking					5111
Ramsey Samuel				1			1	80
Ramsey Thomas				1				
Ramsey Thomas	61	Garrard	Dicks R	1			2	420
Ramsey Thomas L.	115	Garrard	Gilberts Cr	1		1	2	1165

GARRARD COUNTY 1820 TAX LIST

Name	Acreage	County	Water Course	Whites Over 21	Blacks Over 16	Total Blacks	Horses	Total Value
Ray Zackariah	180	Garrard	Sugar Cr	1			4	1600
Reed Jacob								1000
Rice Benjamin				1			2	50
Rice David				1			1	80
Rice Gabrial	150	Garrard	Dicks R	1	1	1	5	2250
Rice George				1	1	5	2	1700
Rice Jacob	175	Garrard	Dicks R	1		2	3	2600
Rice Mary	190	Garrard	Dicks R		2	2	3	
Rice Mary	230	Garrard	Dicks R					
Rice Mary	66	Garrard	Dicks R					6417
Richardson Amos	140	Garrard	Sugar Cr	1	4	5	3	3260
Richardson Baley	30	Garrard	Sugar Cr	1			3	500
Roberson Robert	230	Garrard	Boons Cr	1	1	1	7	4900
Robertson George	32	Garrard	Boons Cr		3	5	3	8750
Robinson Benjamin				1			1	100
Robinson George				1	1	1	3	450
Robinson Henry				1	4	5	6	2210
Robinson Jacob				1				
Robinson James				1			3	150
Robinson James	300	Garrard	Dicks R	1	1	1	3	3800
Robinson James				1		1	2	430
Robinson William				1			1	50
Robinson William				1			1	50
Roman William	65	Garrard	Sugar Cr	1			3	1350
Rosacs Richard				1			2	75
Rose Thomas				1				
Route John	300	Garrard	Dicks R	1	6	18	8	12650
Routz Columbus				1				
Routz Timothy	155	Garrard		1		1	3	1665
Row William	224	Garrard	Dicks R	1	2	7	5	
Row William	15 1/2	Garrard	Dicks R					3422
Salter Michael				1	2	7	2	4500
Sampson Elijah				1			2	135
Santin Elijah					1	1	3	5950
Scott Benlett				1			1	100
Scott James	180	Garrard	Dicks R	1			5	2360

GARRARD COUNTY 1820 TAX LIST

Name	Acreage	County	Water Course	Whites Over 21	Blacks Over 16	Total Blacks	Horses	Total Value
Scott James	195	Garrard	Dicks R	1	3	3	7	3940
Scott John				1				
Scott John D.								
Scott Joseph C.				1			4	180
Scott Joseph J.	59	Garrard	White Oak Cr	1		1	2	970
Scott Joseph Jr.	141	Garrard	White Oak Cr	1	3	8	5	3710
Scott Margaret	119	Garrard	White Oak Cr				2	1250
Scott Nathaniel				1			2	100
Scott William				1			1	90
Scott William Jr				1			1	40
Scruggs Williams	50	Garrard	Gilberts Cr	1	1	2	4	1300
Sellar James	104	Garrard	Sugar Cr	2			8	1350
Shouse Isaac				1			2	100
Shouse William	100	Garrard	Canoe Cr	1				500
Simpson Jesse	51	Garrard	Boons Cr	1			6	735
Simpson John	22 1/2	Garrard	Dicks R	1			1	160
Skiles John				1				
Skiles Malinda							2	100
Smead Alexander	225	Adair	Roaring Lily	2	8	17	14	6500
Smead John	340	Garrard	Dicks R	1	4	7	4	6400
Smead John	216	Adair	Camp Cr					
Smith Absolsom	346	Adair	Camp Cr	1	3	5	11	6060
Smith Edmond Jr.	300	Garrard	Boons Cr	1	2	2	7	4400
Smith Edmund	136	Garrard	Dicks R	1	4	8	5	4440
Smith Ephraim				1			1	75
Smith Henry				1			4	150
Smith James	200	Garrard	Dicks R	1	1	2	2	2670
Smith Jerimiah R.	247	Adair	Camp Cr	1	2	2	9	3875
Smith Jesse	100	Garrard	Clear Cr	1	3	6	7	
Smith Jesse	55	Garrard	Dicks R					3390
Smith John				1	2	3	6	1400
Smith Liberty				1	1	3	3	935

GARRARD COUNTY 1820 TAX LIST

Name	Acreage	County	Water Course	Whites Over 21	Blacks Over 16	Total Blacks	Horses	Total Value
Smith Nancy	20	Garrard	Dicks R					
Smith Samuel	40	Garrard	Dicks R	1	2	6	3	3750
Smith Stone	71	Garrard	Clear Cr	1	1	1	3	1465
Smith Tomsson H.	80	Garrard	Dicks R					1040
Smith William	65	Garrard	Kentucky R	1			1	440
Smithson Thomas				1				
Snate Thomas				1		1	2	600
Spillman Charles	73	Garrard	Dicks R	1	3	4	3	2320
Spillman Charles	213 1/2	Garrard	Dicks R	1	5	12	5	6608
Spillman James	80	Garrard	Kentucky R	1			3	950
Spillman Thomas	130	Garrard	Dicks R	1	3	8	6	4570
Stapp James G.	800	Adair		1		1	1	1700
Steen William Jr.	5 1/2	Garrard	Sugar Cr	1			1	135
Steen William Jr.	100	Garrard	Sugar Cr	1			2	1320
Stemate Charles				1			1	50
Stemate William	70	Garrard	Sugar Cr	1			2	650
Steves Henry	587	Garrard	Sugar Cr	1			2	489
Stevins Edmond				1			4	160
Stewart Joseph				1	4	6	5	2245
Stewart Moses				1			1	50
Stewart Rice L.								
Stewart Robert				1			1	50
Storm Stephen				1	1	1	1	500
Storms Conrad				1			4	200
Strange Washington	160	Garrard	Clear Cr	1	1	1	9	2300
Sutton Alamander				1			2	100
Sutton Benjamin	157	Garrard	Dicks R	1	3	7	3	3842
Sutton Christopher				1				
Sutton Edmond	100	Garrard	Gilberts Cr					2000
Sutton I.	100	Garrard	Dicks R		2	2	2	2000
Sutton James				1			1	50
Sutton John				1			1	40
Sutton Rowland				1	1	1	1	700
Sutton William				1	1	1	2	640
Sutton William	100			1		1	2	1480

GARRARD COUNTY 1820 TAX LIST

Name	Acreage	County	Water Course	Whites Over 21	Blacks Over 16	Total Blacks	Horses	Total Value
Swope Benjamin	145	Adair	Camp Cr	1	5	10	7	5350
Swope Jesse	100	Garrard	Dicks R	1		1	4	2050
Swope John	125	Garrard	Dicks R	1	2	2	2	2960
Swope Margaret	125	Garrard	Dicks R			3		
Swope Samuel				1	1	1	3	680
Tanant Reuben	186	Garrard	Canoe Cr	1	3	6	10	4092
Tatum John				1			2	100
Taylor James	145 1/4	Garrard		1			2	830
Taylor James	250	Garrard	Kentucky R				3	2250
Taylor Jonathan	380	Garrard	Dicks R	1	6	10	13	6740
Taylor Leroy				1			1	50
Taylor Nathan					1	1	2	600
Taylor William C.	350	Madison	Silver Cr	1			2	6250
Terrill Nancy	246	Garrard	Gilberts Cr			1		2460
Terrill Robert	136	Garrard	Sugar Cr	1	1	1	4	1960
Thomas John B.							1	70
Thompson Davis				1			1	75
Thompson James	327	Garrard	Boons Cr	2	8	7	9	
Thompson James	100	Garrard	Boons Cr					
Thompson James	500	Madison	Drowning Cr					
Thompson James	250	Mercer	Chaplin					
Thompson James	237	Franklin	Hammons CR					
Thompson James	5300	Mercer	Salt Cr					
Thompson James	1000	Hardin	Reddy Cr					
Thompson James	500	Madison	Drowning Cr					
Thompson James	506	Madison						
Thompson James	500	Mercer						
Thompson James	500	Mercer						
Thompson James	1500	Mercer						
Thompson James	347	Garrard	Sugar Cr					
Thompson James	500	Garrard						
Thompson James	12	Garrard	Paint Lick					
Thompson James	300	Garrard						20033

GARRARD COUNTY 1820 TAX LIST

Name	Acreage	County	Water Course	Whites Over 21	Blacks Over 16	Total Blacks	Horses	Total Value
Thompson Martha	342	Garrard	Dicks R	1	6	12	5	
Thompson Martha	1000	Clark	Kentucky R					
Thompson Martha	703	Breckenridge	Ohio River					
Thompson Martha	200	Henderson	Ohio River					18050
Thurman Joshua	48	Garrard	Gilberts Cr	1			5	536
Tooley James	106	Garrard	Kentucky R	1			1	348
Tracey Etha	46	Garrard	Kentucky R			2	3	1200
Tracy Elsey				1		1	2	550
Tracy George	200	Garrard	Kentucky R	1	1	1	4	2450
Tracy Sebrit				1			1	100
Tracy William	232	Garrard	Kentucky R	1	2	3	5	3725
Trailor Henry				1			1	75
Trailor Jesse				1				
Trailor Micjah	50	Garrard	Gilberts Cr	1			5	875
Trusmer Phillips	126	Garrard	Boons Cr	1			5	1430
Tungate James				1			1	40
Tungate John	200	Garrard	Sugar Cr	1	1	1	3	2500
Tungate Peter				1				
Tungate Robert				1			1	50
Tungate Royal				1	3	5	3	2100
Turner James	9	Garrard	Kentucky R	1		1	3	600
Turpin Daniel	70 1/2	Garrard	Sugar Cr	1			1	765
Turpin Hezikiah	110	Garrard	Sugar Cr	1	4	8	3	
Turpin Hezikiah	30 1/2	Garrard	Sugar Cr					5284
Turpin Hugh	200	Garrard	Kentucky R	1			2	1580
Turpin James	250	Garrard	Sugar Cr	1	1	1	3	2270
Turpin Thomas	100	Garrard	Sugar Cr	1	1	2	2	1375
Turpin William				1			1	50
Turpin Woodson				1			1	50
Vance Jacob				1			1	50
Vaughn John								
Vaughn Joseph				1			1	50
Walden John	270	Garrard	Dicks R	1	2	5	5	3200
Wall William				1				

GARRARD COUNTY 1820 TAX LIST

Name	Acreage	County	Water Course	Whites Over 21	Blacks Over 16	Total Blacks	Horses	Total Value
Warner Henry				1			1	50
Warner Jacob	73	Garrard	Dicks R	1			2	654
Warner John				1			2	90
Watson Benjamin	550	Garrard	Kentucky R	1	3	4	8	
Watson Benjamin	90	Garrard	Kentucky R					
Watson Benjamin	114	Garrard	Kentucky R					8700
West Charles				1			3	150
West Joseph	100	Garrard	Boons Cr	1	7	17	8	
West Joseph	81	Garrard	Boons Cr					7822
West Lysander				1		2	2	830
West Peyton				1	1	2	2	725
White Benjamin B.				1			1	50
White William				1			1	35
Whitton Elijah				1			3	125
Wilds Benjamin	73	Garrard	Dicks R	1			4	900
Wilds John	46	Garrard	Dicks R	1	1	3	3	1422
Wilmont Samuel					1	1	2	3850
Wilmute Eramus					1	5	2	2250
Wilson Micjah				1				
Wilson Nancy	100	Garrard	Kentucky R		4	8	8	
Wilson Nancy	100	Garrard	Kentucky R					5000
Wilson Nancy	90	Garrard	Sugar Cr				5	1280
Wilson William	100	Lewis		1			1	475
Wither Gideon				1			1	70
Wither Harrison				1			1	75
Withers John	52	Garrard	Kentucky R & Dicks R	1	1	1	2	915
Wood Samuel				1			2	60
Woodruff Joseph					1	2	2	1750
Woods Alvin				1				
Woods John	200	Garrard	Kentucky R	1			3	
Woods John	100	Jessamine						1450
Woods Salley	200	Garrard		1			2	1050
Yager Daniel				1			1	50
Yantis John	264	Garrard	Gilberts Cr	1	5	12	8	
Yantis John	100	Madison	Tates Cr					9950

GARRARD COUNTY 1820 TAX LIST

Name	Acreage	County	Water Course	Whites Over 21	Blacks Over 16	Total Blacks	Horses	Total Value
Young Barney					1	2	5	1050
Young Elizabeth					1	2	5	1450
Young George H.				1				

Garrard County, Kentucky

1828 Tax List

ABBREVIATION LEGEND

R = River

Cr = Creek

LAN = City of Lancaster Kentucky

NIC = City of Nicholasville Kentucky

GARRARD COUNTY 1828 TAX LIST

Name	Acreage	County	Water Course	Whites Over 21	Blacks Over 16	Total Blacks	Horses	Total Value
Adams Abraham	101	Garrard	Long Branch	1		1	2	976
Adams Allen				1			1	60
Adams Elizabeth	50	Garrard	Drakes Cr				2	200
Adams Fethergail	31	Garrard	Sugar Cr	1			5	550
Adams John				1			2	100
Adams John				1			3	50
Adams Judith	400	Garrard	Sugar Cr		4	7	7	4500
Adams Luke	111 1/2	Garrard	Sugar Cr	1	3	5	4	2000
Adams Overton				1			1	30
Adams Walter				1			1	75
Adams Walter	100	Garrard	Sugar Cr	1	5	5	6	2235
Adams William	86	Garrard	Sugar Cr	1		1	6	814
Adcock Benjamin				1			1	30
Alexander Garland				1				
Alexander William	1300	Knox	Robinson Cr	1	2	5	3	2000
Allega James	158	Garrard	Sugar Cr	1			2	554
Allega John	80	Garrard	Sugar Cr	1			3	450
Allen Tobias				1				
Alverson Benjamin				1				
Alverson James		Garrard		1			1	30
Alverson James				1			3	100
Alverson John C	50	Garrard	Sugar Cr	1			1	190
Alverson William				1			1	35
Anderson Archibald	263	Garrard	Drakes Cr	1			5	914
Anderson David	150	Garrard	Drakes Cr	1			1	520
Anderson George				1			2	50
Anderson John	186	Garrard	Paint Lick	1			2	1010
Anderson John	53 1/2	Garrard	Gilberts Cr	1			1	190
Anderson Levi				1				
Anderson Peyton				1			1	40
Anderson Pouncy	46	Garrard	Drakes Cr	1			5	338
Anderson Robert	150	Garrard	Paint Lick	1			3	675
Anderson Simeon H	200	Garrard	Dix R		1	4	8	
Anderson Simeon H	26	Lincoln						

GARRARD COUNTY 1828 TAX LIST

Name	Acreage	County	Water Course	Whites Over 21	Blacks Over 16	Total Blacks	Horses	Total Value
Anderson Simeon H	4 City Lots LAN	Garrard						4731
Anderson Simeon H Heirs	250	Garrard	Sugar Cr		10	23	4	
Anderson Simeon H Heirs	143	Garrard	Boones Cr					
Anderson Simeon H Heirs	40	Garrard	Sugar Cr					
Anderson Simeon H Heirs	20	Garrard	Sugar Cr					
Anderson Simeon H Heirs	1 City Lot LAN	Garrard						12340
Anderson Thomas	104	Garrard	Drakes Cr	1			4	472
Anderson William	250	Garrard	Sugar Cr	2	5	7	8	
Anderson William	260	Garrard	Sugar Cr					
Anderson William	300	Garrard	Sugar Cr					
Anderson William	63	Garrard	Sugar Cr					9900
Anderson William				1				
Arbuchel Drinkard				1			1	35
Arbuchel Stanley				1			1	30
Arnold Elijah	197	Garrard	Paint Lick	1			4	741
Arnold Humphrey	352	Garrard	Back Cr	1	3	4	6	3744
Arnold John	230	Garrard	Paint Lick	1	3	7	9	
Arnold John	44	Garrard	Sugar Cr					
Arnold John	204	Madison	Station Camp					
Arnold John	200	Pulaski	Coon Cr					
Arnold John	200	Pulaski	Forbis Cr					4762
Arnold Thompson				1			1	50
Arnold William				1			1	50
Arvin Alford				1			1	30
Ascew Peterson				1				
Austin David				1			3	120
Austin John				1			1	30
Austin John				1			1	30
Austin Nathaniel				1			2	80
Austin Nathaniel				1				

GARRARD COUNTY 1828 TAX LIST

Name	Acreage	County	Water Course	Whites Over 21	Blacks Over 16	Total Blacks	Horses	Total Value
Austin Preston				1				
Austin Samuel				1			2	120
Austin Thomas				1			1	50
Austin Walter				1			2	50
Austin William				1				
Baines James C	5	Garrard	Paint Lick	1	1	1	1	450
Baker Abraham	103	Garrard	Sugar Cr	1			3	600
Baker Beverly	43	Garrard	Scots Fork	1			2	230
Baker Greenberry				1			1	25
Baker Hence				1			1	50
Baker Henry				1			1	8
Baker John	50	Garrard	Drakes Cr	1			2	150
Baker Joseph				1				
Baker Joseph				1				
Baker Moses	129	Garrard	Drakes Cr	1			2	
Baker Moses	155	Garrard	Drakes Cr					313
Baker William				1				
Baldock Levi				1			1	40
Ballinger Jennings				4	1	2	1	770
Banton George	85	Garrard	Back Cr	1	1	3	2	975
Bartee John				1			2	100
Bassett John				2	5	14	8	3130
Bates Humphrey	200	Garrard	Paint Lick	2			8	650
Bates James				1			3	150
Bates Thomas				1			1	60
Beazley Hiram	65	Garrard	Sugar Cr	1			3	450
Beazley James				1	2	5	7	1195
Beazley James	273	Garrard	Back Cr	1	2	9	3	
Beazley James	180	Wayne	Beaver Cr					4900
Beazley James Jr				1	1	2	4	740
Beazley Roil	283	Garrard	Sugar Cr	1	2	8	6	4289
Bedster John				1			1	45
Beech James	30	Garrard	Sugar Cr	1			1	100
Beeler James				1			3	100
Beeler Perkins				1			1	50
Bell Louis				1			2	50

GARRARD COUNTY 1828 TAX LIST

Name	Acreage	County	Water Course	Whites Over 21	Blacks Over 16	Total Blacks	Horses	Total Value
Bennett James	100	Garrard	Sugar Cr	1			1	560
Berry Milton				1			3	120
Best Ebinzer Jr				1	1	3	13	1380
Best Ebinzer Jr	1300	Garrard	Paint Lick	1	14	29	16	18085
Best James				1	2	11	8	2665
Bicknell Martin	50	Garrard	Back Cr	1	1	1	1	380
Bigz William				1				
Blackwill Robert				1			1	20
Bledsoe A	118	Garrard	Gilberts Cr	1	1	1	2	1860
Bledsoe Alarriah					1	3		500
Bledsoe Margaret	86	Garrard	Gilberts Cr		1	1		1346
Bledsoe Scott	100	Garrard	Gilberts Cr			2	1	1490
Boatwright James				1			2	50
Boatwright James				1			2	50
BoMount Lindsey				1			1	50
Bomount Wesley				1			2	75
Bomount William	240	Garrard	Sugar Cr	1		1	8	1160
Bostick Littlebury				1		1	1	330
Botton John	350	Garrard	Paint Lick	1			1	750
Boyd Andrew				1			2	100
Boyle Alexander	138	Garrard	Back Cr	1	1	1	6	1640
Boyle John	200	Garrard	Back Cr	1	1	6	1	2650
Boyle Robert				1	1	3	2	620
Boyle Rufus				1			1	35
Boyle Rutha	38	Garrard	Back Cr		2	3	3	1320
Bracon Thomas				1			3	150
Brank Robert	214	Garrard	Paint Lick	3	4	6	19	4075
Bratcher Nathaniel L				2	3	4	4	1240
Brawner Noah				1	4	4	2	1000
Brim John				1			1	40
Broaddus Simeon	169 1/2	Garrard	Paint Lick	1	3	4	7	2960
Broadus Thomas	190	Madison	Paint Lick	1			8	885
Brooks John	84	Garrard	Paint Lick	1	1	5	5	1420
Brown A	420	Garrard	Sugar Cr	1	3	5	6	4385
Brown Absalom	130	Garrard	Sugar Cr	1			1	945

GARRARD COUNTY 1828 TAX LIST

Name	Acreage	County	Water Course	Whites Over 21	Blacks Over 16	Total Blacks	Horses	Total Value
Brown Charles	225		Paint Lick	1	2	2	6	2300
Brown George				1		2	3	500
Brown Jacob				1				
Brown Ritchard				1	1	3	2	580
Bruce Elizabeth	60	Garrard	Back Cr		4	5	2	1680
Bruce Jesse				1			1	35
Brumfield James				1			1	40
Bryant Greenbury				1			1	35
Bryant James				1				
Bryant John	85	Garrard	Sugar Cr	1				510
Burton Allen	43 1/2	Garrard	Sugar Cr	1			2	284
Burton John	140	Garrard	Sugar Cr	1			2	990
Burton Patsey					1	2	3	600
Burton Robert				1			1	25
Burton Robert A	52	Garrard	Back Cr	1			3	412
Caret George				1			2	50
Carmel James								
Carpenter Jeremiah	100	Garrard	Fall Lick	1			1	150
Carpenter Reugen				1			1	30
Carpenter Robert	129	Garrard	Paint Lick	1			6	1470
Carpenter Rufus	203	Garrard	Paint Lick	1			5	1824
Carrier Isaac	65	Garrard	Sugar Cr	1			1	
Carrier Isaac	200	Casey	Nob Lick Cr					392
Carter John				1				
Carter John C				1				
Carter Joseph	3 City Lots LAN	Garrard		1	2	4	4	1600
Carter Joseph				1			1	80
Carter Polly					3	5	2	1550
Carver John	215	Garrard	Back Cr	1			3	1390
Casey Stephen	48	Garrard	Drakes Cr	1			4	360
Cheatham Henry				1				
Childers Godsby	96	Garrard	Back Cr	1	1	3	3	1226
Childers Henry	60	Garrard	Sugar Cr	1			2	410
Chrieaman Luke				1			2	30

GARRARD COUNTY 1828 TAX LIST

Name	Acreage	County	Water Course	Whites Over 21	Blacks Over 16	Total Blacks	Horses	Total Value
Clark Abner	57	Garrard	Back Cr	1			4	251
Clark Abner				1			1	35
Clark George & Mother	110	Garrard	White Lick	1			5	480
Clark James				1			2	75
Clark John	40	Garrard	Paint Lick	1			2	160
Clark John				1			1	15
Clark John	130	Garrard	Back Cr	1	2	8	5	2300
Clark William	105	Garrard	Sugar Cr	1	2	2	5	1575
Clements Mattes	54	Garrard	Gilberts Cr	1	2	4	5	1282
Clinton George	110	Garrard	Back Cr	1		1	6	1050
Clouse George H	69	Garrard	Sugar Cr	1			4	238
Clouse William				1			1	35
Cloyd James				1				
Coatney John	252	Garrard	Paint Lick	1	3	7	7	4300
Cockrill William				1			3	75
Colier Alexander	76	Garrard	Scots Fork	1			3	480
Colier Moses	210	Garrard	Paint Lick	1	1	1	12	
Colier Moses	9	Garrard	Drakes Cr					2867
Colier Solomon	133	Garrard	Back Cr	1	1	4	5	1771
Comely James	100	Garrard	Sugar Cr	1			5	800
Comely James	101	Garrard	Sugar Cr	1			2	
Comely James	9 1/2	Garrard	Sugar Cr					674
Comely John				1			1	48
Comely Sabritt	130	Garrard	Sugar Cr	1			5	930
Conn John F				1		1	2	250
Conn John F				1		1	3	300
Conner Caleb				1			2	120
Conner William				1				
Cook Martin				1			1	15
Cook Peyton				1			1	50
Cook Ruban	50	Garrard	Drakes Cr	1		1	4	495
Cook William				1				
Cooke Grove	150	Garrard	Drakes Cr	1			3	720
Crook Sabez	50	Garrard	Drakes Cr	1	1	2	4	570
Crow Mansfield				1				

GARRARD COUNTY 1828 TAX LIST

Name	Acreage	County	Water Course	Whites Over 21	Blacks Over 16	Total Blacks	Horses	Total Value
Crow Patience	106	Garrard	Gilberts Cr		5	7	6	1980
Curtis Peter				1			2	50
Curtis Peter				1			2	60
Curtis Reuben				1			3	100
Dailey Edmond				1			2	60
Dancy Frances				1				
Daniel Edmond	103	Garrard	Paint Lick	1			3	409
David Edward				1				
Davidson Jordan				1			1	40
Davidsson Abner	186	Garrard	Sugar Cr	1	1	1	3	944
Davis Abrham	50	Barren	Dry Cr	1			1	
Davis Abrham	2 City Lots LAN	Garrard						
Davis Abrham	75	Barren						608
Davis Isaac				1			1	17
Davis Samuel	438	Garrard	Paint Lick	2		1	8	2625
Denny George	361	Garrard	Paint Lick	1	8	15	17	7533
Denny James	140	Garrard	Back Cr	1	1	3	10	2225
Denton Josiah	69	Garrard		1	1	2	3	1114
Dentopn John				1			1	20
Dockery Alexander				1			1	40
Dockery George				1			2	50
Dodd Travis								
Dodds James	116 1/2	Garrard	Gilberts Cr	1	2	6	4	
Dodds James	100	Garrard	Harmons Lick					1700
Dollins Jermiah				1			1	50
Dooley Jacob	57	Garrard	Drakes Cr	1			1	
Dooley Jacob	133							300
Dooley Jacob Jr				1			1	40
Dotson Jerimah				1	1	1	1	350
Dotson Jerimah				1	1	1	1	400
Doty Azaniak	275	Garrard	Back Cr	1	3	6	5	3495
Doty Jesse	250	Garrard	Paint Lick	2	1	3	7	2235
Doty John				1	1	1	2	530
Doty Rebecca	358	Garrard	Paint Lick		4	6	5	3736

GARRARD COUNTY 1828 TAX LIST

Name	Acreage	County	Water Course	Whites Over 21	Blacks Over 16	Total Blacks	Horses	Total Value
Dryden James	200	Garrard	Paint Lick	1			7	1400
Dudleston Nelson	33	Garrard	Sugar Cr	1				133
Dudleston William	82 1/2	Garrard	Back Cr	1			3	570
Duff John	125	Garrard	Paint Lick	1			6	525
Duke Henry				1			2	80
Duvall Henry				1				
East Josiah	80	Garrard	Paint Lick	1			2	580
Edminston Joseph				1			1	40
Edminston Thomas				1			1	20
Edwards Elijah				1			1	25
Edwards Garland				1			1	60
Edwards James				1			1	35
Edwards Jesse	115	Garrard	Back Cr	1		3	3	1760
Embry Cader	150	Garrard	Paint Lick	1			2	650
Embry Cader	80	Garrard	Paint Lick	1			1	350
Embry Tartton	60	Garrard	Back Cr	1			3	400
Emebrey (?) Isaac				1			1	30
Endecatt Samuel				1			1	55
Ennis Archibald				1			1	35
Ennis John	5	Garrard	Back Cr	1				100
Evans John				1			2	75
Evans Soloman				1				
Evens Hezekiah	160	Garrard	Sugar Cr	1	5	1	5	1050
Ewing Mathew				1				
Falkner Margarett	678	Garrard	Drakes Cr		2	2	2	2355
Falkner William				1	1	1	2	480
Farice Walker				1			1	40
Faulkner John	100	Garrard	Drakes Cr					600
Faulkner John	367 1/2	Garrard	Paint Lick	1	26	50	51	
Faulkner John	218	Garrard	Paint Lick					
Faulkner John	196	Garrard	Paint Lick					
Faulkner John	145	Garrard	Paint Lick					
Faulkner John	102	Garrard	Paint Lick					24663
Faulkner Peter				1	2	2	9	1010
Faulkner Thomas				1			1	30

GARRARD COUNTY 1828 TAX LIST

Name	Acreage	County	Water Course	Whites Over 21	Blacks Over 16	Total Blacks	Horses	Total Value
Fenton Thomas	68 1/2	Garrard	Long Branch	1			5	885
Ferril Micajah				1		1	1	335
Finnel James	82	Garrard	Paint Lick	1			6	800
Finnell Jonathan	37	Garrard	Paint Lick	1			1	183
Finnell William				1				
Finney Elijah				1				
Fletcher James				1				
Fletcher James	176	Garrard	Back Cr	1	3	3	6	
Fletcher James	48 1/2							2802
Fletcher James (Heirs)	40	Garrard	Paint Lick					120
Fletcher John				1			1	60
Fletcher Thomas	50	Garrard	Sugar Cr	2			3	730
Ford Daniel	100	Garrard	Paint Lick	1		1	4	600
Foster Spencer				1				
Fowler Robert	158	Garrard	Sugar Cr	1	1	1	2	724
Fredenice (?) Joseph		Garrard	Boons Cr	1	1	2		640
Frith Thomas	90	Garrard	Drakes Cr	1				125
Frith Whitton				1			1	25
Gabel William				1			1	30
Gafney John				1			4	200
Gardner James				1			2	100
Gardner William	39	Garrard	Sugar Cr	1			1	200
Garner Thurston				1			1	40
Gates Jacob G.	144	Garrard	Paint Lick	1	2	5	4	1865
Gay James				1				
George James	100	Garrard	Gilberts Cr	1			3	405
Gibbs John	124	Garrard	Back Cr	1				372
Gifford Elijah				1			1	25
Gill James				1				
Gill Joseph	242 1/2	Garrard	Boons Cr		3	6	3	
Gill Joseph	1 City Lot LAN	Garrard						5000
Gill William				1				
Gill William				1			2	120

GARRARD COUNTY 1828 TAX LIST

Name	Acreage	County	Water Course	Whites Over 21	Blacks Over 16	Total Blacks	Horses	Total Value
Goins Myer				1				
Goolsberry Clevers				1			2	80
Graham Enoch	100	Garrard	Gilberts Cr	1	1	3	2	1630
Graves William	269	Garrard	Drakes Cr	1	7	14	6	
Graves William	211	Lincoln	Dix River					
Graves William	90	Lincoln	Dix River					4422
Gray William	1 City Lot LAN	Garrard		1	1	2		800
Green Henry	321	Garrard	Drakes Cr	1	2	4	5	3195
Green Zachariah	130	Garrard	Sugar Cr	1			4	510
Gresham Benjamin	2 City Lots LAN	Garrard			1	1	1	650
Gresham Davis				1			2	50
Grisby William				1			2	80
Gromer Frederick	100	Garrard	Sugar Cr	1				300
Groomer William	262	Garrard	Paint Lick	1			1	826
Gulley Drury	125	Garrard	Paint Lick	1			2	575
Gulley James				1			1	25
Gulley Sqire				1			2	55
Haggard Rice				1			2	60
Hall Anderson				1				
Hall Hiram				1			1	30
Hall Josiah				1				
Hall Josiah				1			1	30
Hall William				1			1	45
Hammach Ephraim				1			2	50
Hammach James	92	Garrard	Sugar Cr	1			1	300
Hammack Ephraim				1			1	25
Hardin George	72	Garrard	Scots Fork	1			2	388
Hardin Robert	47	Garrard	Scots Fork	1			2	263
Harris Elijah				1				
Harris James	100	Garrard	Sugar Cr	1			1	450
Harris James	150	Garrard	Back Cr	1			4	1175
Harris Jesse				1			2	100
Harris Jesse	60	Garrard	Paint Lick	1			3	230
Harris John	106	Garrard	Paint Lick	1	1	2	5	1411

GARRARD COUNTY 1828 TAX LIST

Name	Acreage	County	Water Course	Whites Over 21	Blacks Over 16	Total Blacks	Horses	Total Value
Harris Richmond	170	Garrard	Paint Lick	1				
Harris Richmond	1/2 A		Crab Orchard					720
Harris Robert	150	Garrard	Back Cr	1			1	650
Harris Soloman				1			3	75
Harris Thompason	42	Garrard	Paint Lick	1			5	275
Harris Tyre				1			2	75
Harris Tyre	142	Garrard	Sugar Cr	1	2	4	10	2370
Harris William G	133 1/4	Garrard	Sugar Cr	1			4	779
Harris Willis								
Hays Charles	48 1/2	Garrard	Scots Fork	1			2	239
Heard William				1				
Hedger Samuel	1/2 City Lot LAN	Garrard					1	140
Henderson Alexander	315	Garrard	Paint Lick	1	3	7	13	
Henderson Alexander	50	Madison	Station Camp					4445
Henderson James	186	Garrard	Paint Lick	1	2	3	4	
Henderson James	1250	Madison	Station Camp					2894
Henderson James	106	Garrard	Paint Lick	1			4	796
Henderson James H.				1			1	80
Henderson Robert	83 3/4	Garrard	Paint Lick	1	1	2	5	1435
Henry Richard	100	Garrard	Paint Lick	1			4	600
Henry Robert	182 1/2	Garrard	Paint Lick	2	4	7	7	2342
Hiatt Elijah	633	Garrard	Sugar Cr	1	11	20	16	
Hiatt Elijah	55	Garrard	Back Cr					
Hiatt Elijah	55	Garrard	Gilberts Cr					11694
Hiatt Mary	200	Garrard	Gilberts Cr		3	5	4	1950
Hiatt Reuben	91	Garrard	Sugar Cr	1			4	535
Hiatt Reuben				1			2	85
Hiatt Thomas				1		1	2	200
Hiatt Wilson	138	Garrard	Dix River	1			5	564
Hibbs Jermiah								

GARRARD COUNTY 1828 TAX LIST

Name	Acreage	County	Water Course	Whites Over 21	Blacks Over 16	Total Blacks	Horses	Total Value
Higgenbothem Emanuel	82	Garrard	Paint Lick	2		1	10	
Higgenbothem Emanuel	100	Garrard	Paint Lick					
Higgenbothem Emanuel	266	Garrard	Paint Lick					
Higgenbothem Emanuel	200	Garrard	Paint Lick					3300
Higgenbothem Moses				1			7	350
Higgenbothem Samuel				1		1	2	300
Hill James				1				
Hill Jesse				1			1	25
Hill John	215	Garrard	Sugar Cr	1			3	
Hill John	150	Garrard	Scots Fork					1550
Hill Thomas				1			2	60
Hill Thomas				1			2	60
Hill Zachariah	50	Garrard	Fall Lick Cr					25
Himer Henry				1		1	2	350
Himes Jacob	85	Garrard	Paint Lick	1			3	965
Hogan David				1			2	60
HoHammer Benj.				1				
Hohammer George	134	Garrard	Sugar Cr	1			3	450
Holcomb John	150	Garrard	Paint Lick	1			3	850
Holland John	88	Garrard	Paint Lick	1			2	452
Home Jacob				1			4	300
Homes Edward				1				
Homes Isaac	80	Garrard	Drakes Cr	1			2	210
Homes James	6 1/2	Garrard	Back Cr	1			1	57
Homes Thomas				1			1	
Homes Thomas				1				
Hopper Joseph	4 City Lots LAN	Garrard		2	3	4	1	7520
Hord Frances P.	336	Jefferson	Fishpool Cr	1	5	12	6	

GARRARD COUNTY 1828 TAX LIST

Name	Acreage	County	Water Course	Whites Over 21	Blacks Over 16	Total Blacks	Horses	Total Value
Hord Frances P.	1250	Ohio	Green River					
Hord Frances P.	666 1/2	Ohio	Green River					
Hord Frances P.	1001 1/2	Ohio	Panther Cr					
Hord Frances P.	500	Ohio	Panther Cr					
Hord Frances P.	250	Ohio	Green River					
Hord Frances P.	83	Ohio	Panther Cr					
Hord Frances P.	117 1/2	Ohio	Clover Lick					
Hord Frances P.	3350	Ohio	Jessamine Cr					
Hord Frances P.	8 1/4	Jessamine	Jessamine Cr					
Hord Frances P.	3 Lots in NIC	Jessamine						7289
Hord, Stonestreet & Fishback	495 1/2	Jessamine	Hickman Cr					3468
Horton Anderson				1			2	70
Houchens Frances				1			1	35
Houchens Jesse				1			2	50
Hubbard Joseph	138	Garrard	Scots Fork	1			4	712
Hubbard Moses				1			2	65
Hubbard Saley	100	Garrard	Paint Lick				3	180
Hubbard William	75	Garrard	Scots Fork	1			3	375
Hubbard Wright	40	Garrard	Scots Fork	1			2	240
Hubbard Wright	40	Garrard	Sugar Cr	1			2	205
Hudson Horatio	242	Garrard	Sugar Cr	1	1	7	5	2820
Hughes Isaac	74	Garrard	Paint Lick	1			3	544
Hughes James				1				
Hughes John				1			1	30
Hulett Allen				1			1	40
Hulett John				1				
Hulett Reuben				1			1	40
Hunt Henry				1			2	40

GARRARD COUNTY 1828 TAX LIST

Name	Acreage	County	Water Course	Whites Over 21	Blacks Over 16	Total Blacks	Horses	Total Value
Hunt Smith				1			1	30
Jackson George								
Jameson Barrilla	85	Garrard	Gilberts Cr		1	5	3	1880
Jamison Berrella					2	6	1	1300
Jarvis Moses	16 1/2	Garrard	Gilberts Cr	1	1	2	3	900
Jenkins Thomas					2	3	4	795
Jennings Jesse	50	Garrard	Gilberts Cr	1			1	170
Jennings John					2	5	2	1300
Jennings Samuel	97	Garrard	Drakes Cr	1	1	4	1	616
Jennings William	330	Garrard	Gilberts Cr	1				
Jennings William	20	Garrard	White Oak Cr		6	10	7	
Jennings William	71	Mercer	White Oak Cr					
Jennings William	5 City Lots LAN	Garrard						8931
Johnson Bednego	Free Man of Color						1	20
Johnson Edward	12	Garrard	Drakes Cr	1			1	110
Johnson Edward	12	Garrard	Drakes Cr	1			1	120
Johnson James				1			1	30
Johnson James				1			1	30
Johnson Jane	60	Garrard	Drakes Cr				2	355
Johnson Jane	60	Garrard	Drakes Cr				2	370
Johnson John				1			2	100
Johnson John M.	105	Garrard	Dix River	1	1	2	3	1000
Johnson Thomas				1			2	50
Johnson Thomas				1			1	40
Johnson Washington	115	Garrard	Scots Fork	1			3	790
Johnson William C	84	Garrard	Drakes Cr	1			1	470
Johnson William C	84	Garrard	Drakes Cr	1			2	300
Jones Davis	289	Garrard	Paint Lick	1	3	6	3	2447
Jones John				1	1	1	3	520
Jones William				1			2	100
Jones William								

GARRARD COUNTY 1828 TAX LIST

Name	Acreage	County	Water Course	Whites Over 21	Blacks Over 16	Total Blacks	Horses	Total Value
Joslin Rebecca	240	Garrard	Fall Lick				2	300
Kavanaugh Philmon				1				
Kelley John				1			1	40
Kelley John	165	Garrard	Back Cr	1	2	2	5	650
Kennedy Andrew A.	134 1/2	Garrard	Paint Lick	1			5	1057
Kennedy David	181	Garrard	Drakes Cr	1			2	828
Kennedy David	300	Garrard	Paint Lick	2	5	10	16	4610
Kennedy John	179	Garrard	Paint Lick	1	3	3	8	3272
Kennedy Samuel				1			5	120
Kennedy Samuel	50	Garrard	Paint Lick	1			1	130
Kennedy Samuel				1			3	120
Kennedy Samuel	50	Garrard	Paint Lick	1			1	180
Kennedy Thomas				1	46			
Kerby John Jr.				1			2	40
Kerby Leonard				1			8	200
Kerkendall James	137	Garrard	Drakes Cr	1			2	
Kerkendall James	308	Garrard	Drakes Cr					
Kerkendall James	50	Garrard	Drakes Cr					
Kerkendall James	10 3/4	Garrard	Drakes Cr					
Kerkendall James	100	Garrard	Fall Lick Cr					
Kerkendall James	50	Garrard	Copper Cr					752
Kezer Timothy				1			1	40
Kikendall Richmond	106	Garrard	Paint Lick	1			4	574
Kikindall Jacob	50	Garrard	Drakes Cr	1			2	100
Kiler Joseph	120	Garrard	Sugar Cr	1			2	1060
Kinder William	25	Garrard	Sugar Cr	1			1	155
King Edward				2			4	120
King Mitchell				1				
Kinnaird Ham							1	4500
Kinnaird James				1		3		680
Kirby John				1	1	2	3	600
Knight Robert				1			3	100
Kyler William	50			1			3	550
Lackey Gabrial	461	Garrard	Paint Lick	2	10	21	10	8876
Ladd William				1			3	100
Lair David	90	Garrard	Back Cr	2	3	3	7	1460

GARRARD COUNTY 1828 TAX LIST

Name	Acreage	County	Water Course	Whites Over 21	Blacks Over 16	Total Blacks	Horses	Total Value
Lair George	232	Garrard	Back Cr	1			6	1400
Lair George				1			1	25
Lair James				1			2	65
Lair James				1			6	230
Lair James	204	Garrard	Back Cr	1			5	1016
Lair Jesse	130	Garrard	Sugar Cr	1	1	2	4	1780
Lair William				1	1	3	4	680
Lampton Samuel				1			1	70
Land John				1			2	80
Lane Gelon				1			1	25
Lane James				1			1	50
Lane John					1			
Lane Shedrack				1			2	60
Lane William	56	Garrard	Sugar Cr	1			3	324
Lappan William								
Lapsley William	150	Garrard	Paint Lick	1	1	1	2	1500
Laroless William	150	Garrard	Paint Lick	1			4	900
Lasure William	64 3/4	Garrard	Back Cr	1			3	407
Lawless Peter	40	Garrard	Paint Lick	1			2	200
Lawson John				1				
Lawson William	53	Garrard	Drakes Cr	1	1	3	4	1231
Layton Jerimiah				1			3	100
Layton John	300	Garrard	Paint Lick	1	1	1	7	1910
Layton William				1			1	20
Leasure James				1				
Leasure John	48	Garrard	Drakes Cr	1			1	340
Leasure Joseph	46	Garrard	Sugar Cr	1	1	1	4	918
Leavell Benjamin	255	Garrard	Paint Lick	1	4	7	10	
Leavell Benjamin	125	Garrard	Paint Lick					4813
Leavell John	333 1/2	Garrard	Paint Lick	1	2	4	9	3341
Letcher James H.	400	Garrard	Paint Lick	1	7	17	4	10565
Lewis Thomas				1			2	70
Lillard William	1 City Lot LAN	Garrard						
Littleberry Francis				1				
Locker Jesse	60	Garrard	Paint Lick	1	2	5	3	1385

GARRARD COUNTY 1828 TAX LIST

Name	Acreage	County	Water Course	Whites Over 21	Blacks Over 16	Total Blacks	Horses	Total Value
Logan & Hord	100	Garrard	Paint Lick					
Logan & Hord	777	Garrard	Fall Lick Cr					
Logan & Hord	591	Garrard	Fall Lick Cr					
Logan & Hord	94 3/4	Garrard	Harmon Lick					
Logan & Hord	518	Garrard	Fall Lick Cr					
Logan & Hord	157	Garrard	Fall Lick Cr					
Logan & Hord	50	Garrard	Fall Lick Cr					
Logan & Hord	15 1/4	Garrard	Fall Lick Cr					
Logan & Hord	59 3/4	Garrard	Fall Lick Cr					1565
Logan Hugh	149	Garrard	Paint Lick	1	2	3	3	1695
Logan John	108	Garrard	Back Cr	1		1	7	1020
Logan Timothy	205	Garrard	Paint Lick	1	2	4	3	1895
Loyd Giles				1				
Loyd Hannah	31	Garrard	Sugar Cr				3	246
Loyd Mulky				1				
Lusk Samuel				1			2	160
Lyon Thomas	3	Garrard	Back Cr	1			2	106
Lytle John	355	Garrard	Drakes Cr	1	2	4	7	2925
Manison Robert				1			1	40
Marshall Charles	190	Garrard	Sugar Cr	1			2	622
Mason Elisha	350	Garrard	Fall Lick	2			5	
Mason Elisha	50	Lincoln	Fall Lick					650
Mathews Anderson				1			1	30
Mathews Thomas				1			1	40
Mattingly Richard D.				1			1	20
Maxey Colvit	40	Garrard	Paint Lick	1			1	250
Maxey Samuel	71	Garrard	Paint Lick	1			1	395
McAfee John	170	Garrard	Drakes Cr	1			3	450
McCarley Moses	70	Garrard	Drakes Cr	1		2	2	800
McCoy Alexander				1				
McCoy Hector				1			2	120
McCoy John				1			3	100
McCulley Joseph	80	Garrard	Paint Lick	1			3	400
McCulley Taylor	127	Garrard	Scots Fork	1	1	1	11	1685
McDaniel John				1				

GARRARD COUNTY 1828 TAX LIST

Name	Acreage	County	Water Course	Whites Over 21	Blacks Over 16	Total Blacks	Horses	Total Value
McDaniel William				1			1	35
McDonald James				1			1	75
McDonald William	196	Garrard	Back Cr	1			4	1150
McDonald William	100	Garrard	Back Cr	1			4	782
McDonals William	115	Garrard	Back Cr					690
McFadden James	54	Garrard	Sugar Cr	1			2	345
McFadden James				1			1	35
McFadden William				1				
McKee David L.	1 City Lot LAN	Garrard			4	8	2	2025
McKee Davis	2000	Bath	State Cr					
McKee Davis	1300	Green	Green River					990
McKee Hugh	372	Garrard	Gilberts Cr	2	3	6	8	4090
McMannis Henry				1				
McMannis James				1				
McMannis Nelson	30	Garrard	Sugar Cr	1			1	125
McMannis Washington				1				
McMannis Wayne				1			1	20
McMillan Robert				1			1	50
McMillan William	190	Garrard	Paint Lick	1	1	4	5	2040
McMillin William Jr				1				
McMullins James	121	Garrard	Long Branch	1		2	8	1436
McQuerry Daniel	61 1/2	Garrard	Scots Fork	1			1	224
McQuerry Elizabeth	130	Garrard	Drakes Cr				1	185
McQuerry Joseph				1				
McQuerry William	23	Garrard	Scots Fork	1			2	144
McQuerry William	160	Garrard	Sugar Cr	3	4	11	2	3200
McRamsey (?) Alexander	60	Garrard	Drakes Cr	1			3	270
McVay Hugh				1			3	75
Mennen Abner				1				
Mennifer Willis				1			2	150
Merritt John	360	Garrard	Paint Lick	1	5	16	6	6385
Merritt Margarett	120	Garrard	Paint Lick	1	3	10	1	2600

GARRARD COUNTY 1828 TAX LIST

Name	Acreage	County	Water Course	Whites Over 21	Blacks Over 16	Total Blacks	Horses	Total Value
Middleton William	80	Garrard	Drakes Cr	1			1	230
Miller Daniel	50	Garrard	Drakes Cr	2			2	300
Miller Elizabeth	75	Garrard	Paint Lick		1	2	4	1150
Miller Henry				1	1	2	1	220
Miller John A.	410	Garrard	Back Cr	1	13	31	12	12405
Miller Samuel	11 1/2	Garrard	Gilberts Cr	1	1	2	1	
Miller Samuel	1 City Lot LAN	Garrard						700
Miller Tobias				1				
Miller William	540	Garrard	Paint Lick	1	5	7	7	7600
Minnix Jesse	50	Garrard	Paint Lick	1			1	
Minnix Jesse	50	Garrard	Paint Lick					350
Mitchell Alexander				1			3	75
Mitchell William D	240	Garrard	Paint Lick	1			10	2320
Montgomery James				1			3	100
Moore Moses				1				
Morris Isaac	100	Garrard	Paint Lick	1			1	270
Morris Thomas & Mother				1			1	60
Murphey James	50	Garrard	Sugar Cr	1			1	200
Murphey John				1				
Murphey Polly	100	Garrard	Sugar Cr				1	330
MxClary Franklin	148	Garrard	Paint Lick	1			8	1048
Nailor Edward B.				1			1	250
Nailor George	300	Garrard	Sugar Cr	1	7	9	7	3710
Nailor John	45	Garrard	Scots Fork	1			2	280
Nailor William L.	76	Garrard	Sugar Cr	1		1	2	553
Nicholson Archibald				1			2	50
Nicholson Arthur				1			1	75
Nicholson James	60	Garrard	Drakes Cr	1			4	440
Nicholson James	283	Garrard	Drakes Cr	1			6	1327
Nicholson John				1			1	80
Nicholson John	55	Garrard	Paint Lick	1			2	340
Nicholson Penelope	50	Garrard	Paint Lick		2	4	5	1350
Nicholson William				1			1	60
Nicholson William (Heirs)	130	Garrard	Paint Lick					780

GARRARD COUNTY 1828 TAX LIST

Name	Acreage	County	Water Course	Whites Over 21	Blacks Over 16	Total Blacks	Horses	Total Value
Noel Lunsford R.	50	Garrard	Paint Lick	1			1	260
Noel Rob. C. & Father	113 1/2	Garrard	Paint Lick	2	1	5	6	
Noel Rob. C. & Father	1500	Harlan	Cumberland					
Noel Rob. C. & Father	16	Anderson						2448
Odor Joseph	30	Garrard	Paint Lick	1	1	1	1	550
Odor Thomas	93	Garrard	Back Cr	1			1	540
Oglesby Burgess				1				
Onal John				1			1	45
Padget John				1			2	60
Palmer Hickson	33	Garrard	Paint Lick	1			1	172
Palmer James	77	Garrard	Paint Lick	1	1	1	3	708
Palmer James	312	Garrard	Back Cr	1	2	8	5	4189
Palmer Jesse				1			1	60
Palmer John Jr.	222	Garrard	Copper Cr	1				211
Palmer Nancy	75	Garrard	Back Cr				2	500
Palmer William				1			3	150
Parkinson Joseph								
Parnel Levi				1			1	50
Patterson John	300	Garrard	Paint Lick	1	1	2	15	3455
Payne Ambrose	106	Garrard	Drakes Cr	1			4	418
Payne Ambrose Jr.				1				
Payne Andrew				1			1	30
Payne James				1			1	30
Payne John				1			2	80
Payne Robert				1			2	75
Pennington Burwell				1			1	50
Pennington James				1			2	70
Pennington Newit				1			3	100
Pennington William	52	Garrard	Back Cr	1	1	1	2	950
Perkins Christian	200	Garrard	Drakes Cr	1	3	13	11	4250
Perkins James	100	Garrard	Drakes Cr	1	1	6	5	
Perkins James	300	Cumberland						2245
Perkins John	53	Garrard	Drakes Cr	1			2	355
Perkins John				1			1	30

GARRARD COUNTY 1828 TAX LIST

Name	Acreage	County	Water Course	Whites Over 21	Blacks Over 16	Total Blacks	Horses	Total Value
Perkins John	50	Garrard	Drakes Cr	1			1	240
Perkins Joseph				1	1	4	3	890
Perkins Thomas	60	Garrard	Drakes Cr	1	2	2	4	700
Perring David				1			1	40
Perring Robert	156	Garrard	Gilberts Cr	1			5	980
Petters Ritchard G.				1		1	5	400
Pew Aqiulea				1				
Pierce James				1				
Pierce William				1				
Pinkston John	40	Garrard	Paint Lick	1			2	180
Poe William	80	Garrard	Sugar Cr	1			3	
Poe William	145	Garrard	Sugar Cr					1300
Pointer James				1				
Pointer Jesse	44	Garrard	Fall Lick Cr	1			1	64
Pointer John				1			1	30
Pointer Vincent				1			1	20
Pointer William				1			1	50
Pointer William				1			1	35
Pointer William	76	Garrard	Drakes Cr	1			3	278
Pollard John					3	5	3	1400
Polson Benjamin	117	Casey	Nob Lick Cr	1				
Polson Benjamin	17	Casey	Nob Lick Cr					
Polson Benjamin	300	Casey	Nob Lick Cr					512
Posey Harrison				1			1	50
Posey Price & Mother	192	Garrard	Back Cr	1			3	868
Prater Edward				1			1	40
Prater James	252	Garrard	Long Branch	1	1	4	6	2200
Price William	187	Garrard	Gilberts Cr	1	4	10	8	3731
Pritchard John				1			1	12
Pritchard John				1			1	12
Proctor Benjamin	185	Garrard	Back Cr	1	1	7	5	3350
Proctor John				1			1	50

GARRARD COUNTY 1828 TAX LIST

Name	Acreage	County	Water Course	Whites Over 21	Blacks Over 16	Total Blacks	Horses	Total Value
Pugsh John				1			1	40
Pullins Mathews	153 1/2	Garrard	Paint Lick	1	1	3	5	1450
Puring Charles				1				
Quinn Abalom	100	Garrard	Gilberts Cr	1		3	4	
Quinn Abalom	30	Garrard	Gilberts Cr					1600
Rainey John				1			1	80
Rainey William				1			4	210
Ray Daniel	187	Garrard	Sugar Cr	1	1	2	2	1211
Ray Eli	85	Garrard	Paint Lick	1			2	495
Ray Jefferson	95	Garrard	Sugar Cr	1	1	3	1	900
Ray Michael	237	Garrard	Sugar Cr	1			4	841
Reece John	50	Garrard	Paint Lick	1			1	50
Renfro William	195	Garrard	Paint Lick	1	1	1	4	
Renfro William	200	Garrard	Paint Lick					2425
Rentfro Isaac	107	Garrard	Drakes Cr	1			2	391
Rentfro Thomas				1				
Richardson Surana	147	Garrard	Gilberts Cr		1	1	4	1200
Rigdon Frances	70	Garrard	Sugar Cr	1			1	110
Rigsby Robert				1			1	15
Rigsby Robert				1			1	12
Robards Nathaniel				1				
Rogers John				1			2	70
Rogers Travice				1			1	30
Ross Elizabeth	250	Garrard	Drakes Cr		3	9	6	
Ross Elizabeth	100	Garrard	Drakes Cr					
Ross Elizabeth	200	Madison	Silver Cr					3980
Ross Elizabeth	250	Garrard	Paint Lick		3	9	7	
Ross Elizabeth	100	Garrard	Fall Lick Cr					
Ross Elizabeth	250	Garrard	Silver R					3780
Ross Robert				1				
Ross Robert				1				
Ross Thomas	300	Madison	Silver Cr	1			1	380
Ross Thomas	300	Madison	Silver R	1			1	350
Rothwell Gideon				1			2	100
Rowland Morgan				1				
Rowton Thomas	75	Garrard	Back Cr	1	2	6	4	1875

GARRARD COUNTY 1828 TAX LIST

Name	Acreage	County	Water Course	Whites Over 21	Blacks Over 16	Total Blacks	Horses	Total Value
Royston William	211	Garrard	Back Cr	2	7	11	11	
Royston William	121	Garrard	Sugar Cr					
Royston William	475	Madison	Otter Cr					7658
Rungon Asa				1				
Rutherford George	134	Garrard	Drakes Cr	1	1	1	1	500
Sadler Edward	209	Garrard	Paint Lick	1	4	9	3	3345
Sanders James	132 1/2	Garrard	Paint Lick	1			3	630
Sartain Elijah	199	Garrard	Boons Cr	1	5	11	10	
Sartain Elijah	3 City Lots LAN	Garrard						12300
Shackelford Ryland				1			3	80
Singleton Abel				1			1	30
Singleton Allen				1				
Singleton John	430	Garrard	Drakes Cr	1			1	1344
Smith James	1 City Lot LAN	Garrard		1	2	4	1	1840
Stiger James	60	Garrard	Drakes Cr	1	2	2	7	1180
Storms (?) William				1	1	1	4	265
Storms William				1				
Wheeler John	93	Garrard	Scots Fork	1			2	432
Wheeler William	415	Garrard	Back Cr	1	7	15	7	5135
Williams Thomas	127	Garrard	Paint Lick	1	4	7	4	
Williams Thomas	300	Pulaski	Brush Cr					2522
Wilmont S. S.	49	Garrard	Drakes Cr	1	2	3	2	2900